JEWELS OF THE BIBLE

Iconic Stories Passed Down from Parent to Child
Through the Generations….

DIANNA BLAKE DAVIS

Library of Congress Control Number: 2013923842
CreateSpace Independent Publishing Platform
North Charleston, South Carolina

To Tabatha, Travis, Brianna, Michael, and Elijah, my beautiful children. I love you more than you will ever know.

A MESSAGE FROM THE AUTHOR

God's love for all of us is truly amazing! Personally, I can tell you that His love has not only carried me through the worst of times but has also blessed me with the most joyful memories of my life. There is nothing that I desire more than for children, young and old alike, to learn about God's love for them.

As a descendant of the author William Blake, God blessed me with the gift of creative writing. Realizing this, I wanted to do something with my gift to spread the good word by sharing stories of God's great love, forgiveness, and salvation for his children. As I began re-writing each of these stories, I felt God guiding me line by line to accurately re-tell these 14 lessons that are pillars of the Christian faith, while He was always reminding me to 'keep it fun.' Loving Dr. Seuss as a child, I wanted to retell Bible stories so that children can anticipate the rhyming endings and get caught up in the excitement of the stories.

It is my hope that your children, grandchildren, and great-grandchildren, enjoy their time with you as you read these stories to them and that this book is passed down in your family from one generation to the next.

With love,

Dianna Blake Davis

INTRODUCTION

Jewels of the Bible is a collection of iconic Bible stories embracing the themes of courage, compassion, redemption, faith, and God's love for people from all walks of life. Prepare your hearts and minds. These stories are written in an exciting and rhythmic style that is easy to understanding and fun to read.

Passed down from parent to child through the generations, you can now enjoy reading these amazing stories of men and women from the Old and New Testament, who lived out these adventurous lives long, long ago.

CONTENTS

STORY OF NOAH

STORY OF NOAH

In the time of Noah, life increased greatly on the face of the Earth.
God saw it was corrupt and wicked, nothing of value or worth.

Noah heard God tell him all life on Earth would soon end.
Mankind was corrupt with wickedness. It wasn't as he planned.

The sons of God saw the daughters of men were fair and were admired.
They took as their wives from these daughters, any that they desired.

This offspring made the Nephilium, the renowned mighty men of old—
The famous giants with super powers, of whom legends are told.

The Earth was full of evil, and violence in the hearts of man.
God was grieved that they were ever made. He planned to destroy them.

Noah and his wife had three sons: Japheth, Ham and Shem.
Noah walked and found favor with God because he was a righteous man.

God instructed Noah to build an Ark, made out of gopher wood.

"Three stories high you shall make it Noah," God's instructions were understood.

"All life saved inside the Ark, I will make my covenant with you.
Your family Noah I will save, your wife and your sons' wives too."

"You shall gather all the living animals. You will take two of every kind.
As they come, put them in the Ark to make sure that they survive."

"I will wipe off from the face of Earth every creature I have made."
He then told Noah, "Go enter the Ark for I AM sending rain in seven days."

"Male and female clean and unclean will come to stay alive—
Birds and cattle every creeping thing, each after their own kind."

Two by two the animals came, Noah assigned each to their pen.
Noah and his family were told stay inside, and then God shut them in.

All safe in the Ark escaping death, when the springs of the great deep burst forth.
The floodgates of Heaven were opened, and the rain fell hard on the Earth.

Gone, all with the breath of life, all that breathed with its

nostrils died.
The water increased and the ark lifted up, wiping out mankind.

Noah was six hundred entering the Ark, together with his sons and their wives.
Noah did all God commanded. Then it rained forty days and forty nights.

One hundred and fifty days the Ark floated on the surface of the Earth.
Noah sent out a Raven to check, but it just flew back and forth.

God remembered Noah and sent a strong wind to dry the ground.
The Seventeenth day of the Seventh month the Ark came resting down.

Resting on Mt. Ararat as the water continued to recede,
The first day of the tenth month the mountain tops could be seen.

Noah then sent out a dove. It came back, still no place to land.
The next time it came back and placed an olive leaf in Noah's hand.

Then God told Noah, "Come out of the Ark, for the ground is completely dry.
Now turn loose every living creature also, so they can go forth and multiply."

The dove returns to Noah's ark bringing an olive leaf. The olive leaf
is a sign that the waters have gone down and that there is land again.

"When clouds come I make a promise Noah -- I will never flood Earth again.
My rainbow I now place in the sky, as my covenant made with man."

THE WALLS OF JERICHO

THE WALLS OF JERICHO

Now it came to pass that Joshua had come back to Jericho again.
Behold he saw a man standing, with a great sword drawn in his hand.

Joshua then approached him, because he had to ask and see.
"Are you for us, on our side? or are you for our enemies?"

"I AM the commander of heaven's armies I'm not on either side.
But as the LORD of the heavenly forces, I have now arrived!"

The LORD said "Take off your sandals. You are standing on holy ground.
Joshua did so bowing low, in reverence he fell facedown.

The LORD said to Joshua, "See, I have given their mighty men right into your hand."
Jericho was shut down because of Israel. No one coming in or out of the land.

LORD said "For the next six days, you'll march 'round the city with all your men of war.
"With seven priests going before the ark, with trumpets made of ram's horn."

"On the seventh day, seven times, you will march around the city walls."

The LORD appears to Joshua outside the walls of Jericho
commanding him to bow and to follow His orders.

"Priests sound trumpets, Israel shouts and the walls of Jericho will fall!"

Joshua told the people everything the LORD said to do.
"Priests, take up the ark of the covenant. We will do as we are commanded to!"

Joshua instructed the people, "Don't let a word come out of your mouth!
"Until the day you are told, and then you shall shout a Great Shout!"

They marched once around the city, the next six days with all their men of war.
Seven priests going before the ark, with seven trumpets made from rams' horn.

On the seventh day they rose early, at dawn they rose with the sun.
That seventh day they marched around the city seven times.
The victory was mightily won!

The sound, a Great Shout! and trumpets blowing. Jericho's walls they fell!
So when Israel went into the city, every man's footpath was leveled.

Joshua's instructions regarding Rahab the harlot: "All in her house let them live!
When we came here to spy land, we were safe in her house, as we were hid."

When Israel saw victory, they shouted out with one accord.
Jericho the city, all the silver and gold were made Holy
and kept for the LORD.

The people of Israel celebrate and shout great shouts of
victory as the walls of Jericho fall.

BOAZ AND RUTH

BOAZ AND RUTH

In the land of the Judges, a long time ago,
A family from Bethlehem left the land that they owned,

In search of new fields. For the famine severe,
Settled in Moab. Then after 10 years,

Her husband and both sons had been taken away.
Naomi stricken with grief, her heart in dismay.

Her sons were both gone now, so she longed to return.
To the place of her homeland, the place of her birth.

She heard God had blessed her land once again.
She told her daughter in-laws goodbye, and that she loved
them.

"May the LORD bless you, as you both are still young.
"I am much too old now, to bear you more sons."

Naomi cried aloud, kissed them and said goodbye.
Ruth said, "No, I will not go. I will stay by your side."

"I will go with you, to your land abroad,
Your people my people, your God be my God."

"Where you sleep, I sleep. Where you stay, I stay.
I want to be with you. Don't send me away."

So they packed up and went, back to her own land.

Boaz sees Ruth for the very first time as she's gathering
barley in the fields.

The harvest was just beginning in Bethlehem.

Now the whole town was stirred as Naomi returned home.
With her daughter in law Ruth, she wasn't alone.

Ruth said to Naomi, "Let me go to the fields.
I'll glean in behind them, to make us a meal."

"Go now my daughter, and do as you say."
That is where Boaz, saw her that very first day.

Kinsman redeemer, a man of great wealth,
From Elimelech's family, owned some ripe barley fields.

Boaz came upon the field in the middle of the day, asked his worker,
"Who was this maiden, who had traveled his way?"

"She asked to come gather, after they glean.
She has worked from this morning, a little rest in between."

Boaz said, "Listen my daughter, in this place you can yield.
Take all you need, you must not leave this field."

"I feel you'll find danger, stay under my cover.
Do not go and glean, in the fields of another."

"Stay close to my maidens. Watch where they go."
I've told the men not to touch you, let this be so."

"When you thirst, drink cool water, the young men bring around."
Ruth was filled with joy, at the favor she had found.

Ruth asked, "Why this great kindness, I have found in your sight?"
I will do as you say, if you say it is right."

He answered, "It's the God of Israel, under His wings you have come.
Our God will recompense you fully, for all the good you have done."

Through the day he did watch her, he would give her a smile,
"Dip your bread in the oil, child, now come refresh for a while."

She ate till she was full, and had more besides.
She would save for Naomi, she thought with a smile.

Boaz told the reapers, to leave sheaves to lie.
Handfuls on purpose, just leave them behind.

She gathered till evening, then on the threshing floor, an Ephod of barley, perhaps even more!

Ruth went home. Naomi asked, "Child, where did you glean?"
She answered, "In the field of Boaz! I've found favor it seems."

Naomi said, "This man is a kinsman, with the right to redeem!
Blessed be the LORD God who has made you, highly esteemed!"

Ruth replied, "He told me to stay, until the harvest is complete.
Stay with his maidens, to glean barley and wheat."

Naomi said, "Wash, anoint yourself, and put on your best clothes.
Go down to the threshing floor, but don't make your self known."

"Do as I say daughter, and at the twilight,
Boaz will be, on the threshing floor tonight."

"After he eats and drinks, see where he goes.
Make sure you are hidden, so nobody knows."

"He will tell you what to do, to make this complete.
When he lays, you will go down and uncover his feet."

Boaz woke in the night, saw her lying there.
"I am Ruth your maidservant. I've come under your care."

He said, "Daughter fear not. I will do this task.
Everyone knows you are decent and brave, and worth more than you ask."

Boaz asks Ruth to stay with his maidens, who are the
women who work for him.

"It is true, I am your kinsman, but there is one, closer still.
If he will not redeem you, then surely I will."

He packed her up with barley and sent her away.
Naomi said he will not sleep, it will be settled this day.

He saw the kinsman he was seeking, walking his way.
"Please come over and talk. I have something to say."

With the elders at the gate, all the witnesses came near,
Explained all the requirements, his intentions made clear.

He said, "I cannot redeem. I have my own wife to handle.
Redeem it for your self, then Boaz took off his sandal."

Boaz said, "At the gate of his birthplace, you all witness this day.
All that is owned by Elimelech, the price for it, I will pay."

"All that Naomi has, I will restore."
Ruth married him and handed him the son she had bore!

Boaz, father of Obed,
Father of Jesse, who bore the great King David!

THE ANOINTING
OF DAVID

THE ANOINTING OF DAVID

The LORD asked Samuel, as his heart was torn.
"How long now Samuel will you continue to morn?"

God said, "I have rejected Saul as Israel's king
You must trust this. I AM doing a brand new thing."

"Fill your horn with oil and be on your way!
I'm sending you to Jesse in Bethlehem this day."

"For I have found my new king among Jesse's sons.
Hurry now and go and I will tell you which one."

Samuel was afraid and asked, "How can I go?
"If Saul hears he will kill me. You know this is so."

"Tell him you will sacrifice in the name of the LORD.
Take a heifer with you and give them this word."

"Invite Jesse the Bethlehemite I will tell you what to do.
You shall anoint for me whom I tell you to!"

Samuel obeyed this order given to him.
And made his way along down to Bethlehem.

The elders of the town trembled, asked, "Are you coming in peace?"
Samuel said "I am coming to sacrifice we will have a great feast!"

"Now go and consecrate yourselves, and then come with me."
He told Jesse, "Bring all your sons down, individually."

First came to Jesse, Eliab, eldest son.
Samuel thought surely God has anointed this one.

The LORD told Samuel, "No, don't be deceived
By appearance or stature, that's not as the LORD sees."

"Look not on the outside but look at the heart.
It's not the outside but the inside that sets them apart."

Abinadab and Shammah passed, yet none chosen still.
Jesse said, "There is my youngest son, but he is out in
the field."

"He tends to the sheep, but I will send for him now.
Samuel said, "Send for him. We will not eat till he sits
down."

Jesse then brought David, a boy with beautiful eyes,
A fine looking boy. The LORD said, "Do not consider his
size."

The LORD told Samuel, "Arise and anoint him for this is
He!"
As the spirit of God fell on David mightily.

Samuel took the horn of oil, poured on David's head,
In the midst of all his brothers, and then all were fed.

From that day forward God would provide
Protection for David and blessings beside.

The spirit of God then departed from Saul.
An evil spirit entered. He could not hear God at all.

He was tormented and troubled inside his head—
No direction, no spirit of God to be lead.

Samuel anoints David as the chosen one of the
LORD amongst his brothers.

"Let the king now command for your servants to hire,
A man skillful with music, the harp and the lyre."

"When the evil spirit comes upon you, music he will play—
It will make you well, make the evil go away."

"I have seen David, Jesse's son, an attractive young boy.
He plays skillfully. Him we can employ."

Saul said, "Find a man who plays well and bring him to me.
Send for the son of Jesse if he plays eloquently."

"The LORD is with him. He displays courage without fear."
Saul said, "Go get him and bring him here."

Saul sent word to Jesse, "Send David who is tending the sheep,
To play some music so that I can find sleep"

Jesse packed up a Donkey and sent David away.
He was now in the service of Saul for the music he would play.

Loaded with bread and skins of fine wine,
David went before the King for the very first time.

David came to serve Saul and found favor in his heart.
David played the harp well and the evil spirit did depart.

Saul sent a message to Jesse, "Please let David stay.
When the evil spirits come upon me, David plays them away."

When King Saul felt burdened by evil spirits, David
played the harp for him so the King could find rest.

DAVID AND GOLIATH

DAVID AND GOLIATH

Israel's army on one Mountain, the Philistines were on the other.
With the Valley of Elah between them, they could scream and yell at each other.

The Philistines had a giant. His name was Goliath of Gath,
Covered in armor made of bronze, with a heavy spear in his hand.

Before Goliath walked his armor bearer, holding a heavy bronze shield.
The giant stood each day screaming, "Send a man, we'll fight in this field."

"If he is able to kill me, then we'll be your slaves.
If not you will work for us" (the same argument made forty days).

Then came a boy named David, from the town of Bethlehem.
Son of Jesse the Ephrathite, descendent of Abraham.

This Jesse had eight sons, three of whom followed King Saul.
David's job was to care for the flocks. He was the youngest of them all.

Ephah of grain, ten loaves of bread and take ten cheeses beside.

Jesse packed up David, to carry all of his brothers' supplies.

David rose up early and took off with the provisions.
Jesse said, "Leave the sheep and bring back news of your brothers' condition."

David hurried to the encampment, when he heard the battle cry.
He left packages with the keeper and left to find out why?

David found and greeted his brothers, asked them, "Why are you so terrified?"
They said, "Behold this giant Goliath, have you ever seen a man of this size?"

Israel's army was fleeing, they seemed totally afraid.
Then David saw Goliath and Israel's warriors run away!

David said, "It is the armies of the living God that this man defies!"
"Brothers, what shall be done for one who kills this Philistine?"

He asked again the question, why none would face this man.
He'd have riches with no taxes, and King Saul's daughter's hand!

Eliab, David's brother, this was Jesse's eldest son,
Burned with anger at David's questions, and asked him why he'd come!

"Why don't you just leave now, and go finish up your chores?
Why is it that you came here and left those few sheep of

yours?"

Well David was not afraid, told King Saul that he would fight.
He said, "Do not let your hearts be afraid I will go and make this right."

Saul said, "No you are just a boy and I must tell you the truth.
You are no match for this giant who had been trained up from his youth."

David said, "My father's sheep I have kept safe, from both lion and bear."
When they rose up against me, I caught them by the hair."

"God gave back the lamb to me, out of the lion's jaws!
The LORD who delivered me, from both bear and lions' paws."

"God will do the same again! This victory will be mine.
He has defied the Living God! This uncircumcised Philistine."

Saul told David "Go ahead and try if you think you can."
David knew the LORD would give Goliath into his hands.

Saul said, "To give you some protection help shelter you from harm,
Why don't you go ahead and put my armor on."

David tried to wear it, but had to take it off.
He said, "I'm just not used to this, and went to look for some rocks."

Five smooth stones he spotted—shining on the ground.
He stuck four in his shepherd's pouch, and in a sling slung one around.

Goliath looked and saw David and thought this was some trick.
He said, "What am I a dog that you come at me with a stick."

Goliath said to David, "If you come here you will be killed.
I will feed your body to the birds and beasts of the field."

David yelled, "God has a word for all you who are gathered here.
God wants you to know that He saves not with sword and spear."

David shouted, "You come to me in armor with spear and Javelin,
But the battle is the LORD'S and He will give you into our hands."

David took out a smooth stone and placed it in his sling.
He swung and swung it all around till it went barreling.

Sinking in his forehead, Goliath crashed to the ground.
Falling slowly to the earth, this giant came tumbling down.

David took the giant's sword and cut off Goliath's head.
The Philistines then ran in terror to see their champion dead.

After David kills Goliath with a stone from his
sling, he approaches the dead giant to take his
sword as the Philistines run away in fear.

BOOK OF ESTHER

BOOK OF ESTHER

The 3rd year King Xerxes reigned upon the throne.
Days of celebration, inviting all of the well-known:

The nobles and princes, the highly acclaimed,
The upper elite, holding honor and fame.

Then after the 180 days were complete,
The people's banquet was held, invited, the rich to the least.

In golden goblets with royal wine,
Everyone was having a wonderful time!

In the Garden Palace, the food was delicious,
Showing off his Majesty's treasures and riches.

For the women Queen Vashti was hosting a feast,
In the Royal household, that belonged to the King.

On the seventh day, the King was merry with wine.
He sent his Servants, to go out and find,

Queen Vashti so fair, her beauty renowned,
To appear to the King, wearing her Royal Crown.

Vashti refused, to come at his command,
In his rage, the King consulted with the other men.

They said, "You must send out, a Royal decree."
What must be done to one, who has wronged the King?"

"From Persia to Media, send it forth:
'Vashti will come before the King, no more!'"

"'Her royal position, give to one better still—'
A law that cannot be changed, here sign with your royal seal."

"The deeds of Queen Vashti will become well known,
Wives will honor their husbands. Respect must be shown."

Then after these things, The King's wrath was appeased.
He soberly recalled Vashti and what he decreed.

Those who were there created the plan,
To gather the beautiful virgins, from all the land.

All beautiful maidens, to be brought to the King,
To replace Vashti and to crown a new Queen.

Now the Jews were in exile and carried away,
By Nebuchadnezzar and many were slain.

Many lost parents and were raised by kin.
That's where our story of Esther begins.

There was a Jew named Mordecai, the son of Jair,
He raised his niece Hadassah, who had come under his care.

Hadassah, now called Esther, was also taken away,
To the harem palace, under guard, now with law's decree.

The keeper of the women, taken from all the lands.
Were all received by Hegai, and under his full command.

Esther was a beauty, lovely and so fair.
She found favor with Hegai, For her beauty was very rare.

He moved Esther to the best location,
After the days of her purification.

Six months of sweet spices, and six months of Myrrh.
Expensive oils were lavished on her,

She had the best place in the harem, with the very best view.
From the palace, seven maidens were given her too.

Mordecai was an attendant, who worked inside the court,
Each day he walked by the harem, to get a full report.

Mordecai told Esther, "Now until you find your place,
Hadassah you must be Esther. Do not tell them of your race!"

Now when the time was given, for each girl, one night with the King.
The royal treasury was open to them. They could choose from everything!

Now the time had come for Esther, to come before the King.
She required nothing except the things that Hegai did bring.

Now Esther won everyone's favor, with her beauty and her grace.
The King loved her more than any other. He saw the beauty in her face.

He took her hand in his hand, as he walked and gently lead.

He said I'll give you a kingdom, set a royal crown upon her head.

Then the feast of Esther, giving the people their new Queen,
Lowering taxes, giving gifts, showing great generosity.

Now at this time Mordecai, was sitting at the nobles' gate.
He overheard two officers, with plans to assassinate.

Mordecai told Queen Esther, what they were going to try.
Investigation found it to be true, credit given to Mordecai.

Recorded in the annals, by the scribe, and penned in ink.
This day Mordecai the Jew, did save the life of the King.

Then came Haman the Agagite, a crafty man with evil report.
Was given position by the King, even highest in the court.

And to show all his great authority, A royal ring placed upon his hand.
All the princes, were to bow to him. Every noble in the land.

Because Mordecai did fear his God, and would not fall upon his face,
Wicked Haman devised an evil plan, to destroy the Jewish race!

Oh King, there are a certain people, with laws different from your own.
Who will not show respect for you, and they must be overthrown.

10,000 talents of silver, and treasures to be brought before the

King.
A law that cannot be undone, it must be sealed with your signet ring.

Together they threw lots to find out, exactly when to start.
Sent letters by special messenger, set for the 12th day of Adar.

When Mordecai read the edict, with the orders put in place,
He put on sackcloth and ashes, wailed out loudly at the King's Gate.

None in sackcloth and ashes, could come inside the court.
Esther sent out clothes for him, and asked to get a full report.

Queen Esther's servants told her, something's wrong with Mordecai!
He is sitting in sackcloth and ashes, crying out loudly and said this is why:

They handed her the letter, it read "Every Jew to be killed."
Set for the 12th day of Adar, the decree it was signed and was sealed.

After Esther read a copy of the edict, she was exceedingly distressed and dismayed.
In the note Mordecai said, "you must go to the King that you might save your people this way."

"Deliverance will come if you stay silent. Don't think you are safe and will miss.
Who knows if you have come into the Kingdom? Queen Esther for such time as this!"

She said, "If I perish I perish. I cannot sit here and not even try.
I will go to the King uninvited, even if it means my demise."

She asked Mordecai, "Do one last thing, ask the people to please fast and pray."
Mordecai said he would and then he walked away.

After three days, dressed in royal robes, Esther came into the court.
The King saw her standing and said, "Queen Esther, please come forth."

"Touch the end of the golden scepter and I will hear your plea.
Even to half of the kingdom I will give to thee."

She touched the Golden Scepter. She obtained favor in his sight.
She knew God was with her and things would be alright.

"I request that you come for a dinner I have prepared for you my King.
And summon Haman also. Bring him along with you please."

The King sent for Haman, ordered him get ready and come.
So all that Queen Esther requested, for her would quickly be done.

Then after the wine was served, the King asked her one time more.
"Even to half of the kingdom, Queen Esther ask and it is

yours."

Queen Esther said, "If I have found favor, and if you think
that it is right,
Let the King and Haman come again for dinner tomorrow
night."

Haman went away elated, the joy was full within his heart.
The King and Queen called on him alone, with the honor to
take part.

But then Haman saw Mordecai, who refused to show any
fear.
Haman angrily walked away, thinking, "Mordecai's end is
near!"

Once home with his wife and friends Haman retold them all
the stories:
How the King had given him riches and great authority.

"Yet all this benefits me nothing, as long as I still see
Mordecai."
His friends said, "Let a gallows be made for him, 50 cubits
high."

This thought pleased Haman greatly! And he ordered to have
it made.
"I'm going to get the King's consent, to hang Mordecai right
away."

On that night the King could not sleep. He turned and tossed in his bed.

He ordered the Chronicles of memorable deeds and current events to be read.

King Xerxes orders the Chronicles of memorable deeds and current events to be read to him and discovers that Mordecai had stopped a plot to kill the King.

It read that two of the King's royal guards had been ordered to die.
A plot found out and put to a stop by the good guard Mordecai.

Bigthana and Teresh planned to kill the King.
This day Mordecai the Jew, did save the life of the King.

Xerxes asked what happened and what was the reason why?
"You say he saved my life, this man named Mordecai?"

"Isn't he the Jew that works down at the King's gate?
No honor or recognition distinctions have been made?"

"Sire no, I'm sorry there is nothing here to report."
Just then Haman was spotted entering in the inner court.

King asked, "What is to be done for the one in whom the King delights?"
Haman said, "We must think about this, to be sure to get this right."

"Sing his praises to the people. Walk him through the public square.
And a horse ridden by the King, sit him on your royal mare."

Dress him in fine robes and put a crown on his head.
In purple and in linen by a noble he will be lead."

Haman said, "I am honored and if you think it is right,
This is what will be done for the one in whom the King delights!"

The King said, "Leave out nothing you have spoken and make haste.
All this do for Mordecai the Jew, who works at the King's gate."

So Haman took the King's garments and put on Mordecai a crown,
Loudly proclaiming the King's delight, as he paraded Mordecai around.

Mordecai is honored by the King by being dressed in fine robes and a crown as Haman parades him through the streets proclaiming the King's praises of his heroic deed.

After Mordecai was finished Haman went home covering his head.
The attendant came quickly to take him to the dinner Esther had prepared.

They came in to dine again, and when the wine was served,
"What is your request Queen Esther? Tell me so you can be heard."

Queen Esther said, "If I please the King, if you think it is right,
Let my life be given to me and my people this night."

"Destroyed and wiped out of existence, with a decree we have been sold,
For 10,000 talents of silver and all of our treasures and gold."

"If we had merely been sold as slaves, I would have held my tongue.
Our affliction is nothing compared to the damage to you would be done."

"Who is this that would dare presume, in his heart to do such a thing?"
"An adversary and an enemy," she said, "this wicked Haman my King."

Haman was afraid. He stood up then fell on the couch.
"Will he even assault my wife and Queen in my presence and my house?"

Just then the attendants came in and told, "Gallows 50 cubits high,

In the yard of Haman built, for the good guard Mordecai."

The King said put Haman on it and took the ring off of his hand.
Esther had just saved her people. She became beloved in the land.

Esther then told Xerxes that to her, Mordecai was kin.
Mordecai took Haman's position, then their new life did begin.

Haman pleads with Queen Esther to spare his life.

THE WRITING
ON THE WALL

THE WRITING ON THE WALL

King Belshazzar, son of Nebuchadnezzar reigned on the throne.
He hosted a feast in the presence of thousands, and ordered the vessels of gold,

So his concubines nobles and wives might drink their wine out of them.
Golden Goblets from the royal treasury, Nebuchadnezzar stole from Jerusalem.

From Holy of Holies in the temple of God, vessels crafted in silver and gold
Were brought in to worship with their foreign gods, made from bronze, wood, iron and stone.

Across from the light of a candlestick, in a room clearly visible to all,
Suddenly appeared fingers of a man writing something on the wall.

The King himself saw the back of the hand. The writing was plain to see.
Just then, the King's countenance fell. He turned pale and knocked in the knees.

The King cried, "Bring the soothsayers out. Send for the wise men to come."
Who ever can tell me what this writing is, and give the interpretation thereof,"

During King Belshazzar's great banquet the hand of a man
mysteriously appeared on a wall and began to write a message.

"A gold chain I will put around his neck, dress him in purple and linen.
I will give him authority, even third highest in the kingdom."

The wise men came, but could not make known, the interpretation to the king.
The King now terrified, he grew pale, wondering what could this mean.

"May the king live forever! Don't be afraid, my son don't look so pale!"
The Queen Mother came in after hearing the voices to understand in all detail.

She said, "There is a man in this kingdom with understanding. He can tell you what this means.
With wisdom and knowledge, handles difficult problems with ability to interpret dreams."

"The man named Daniel, who your father called Belteshazzar, would be the one to come.
Anytime when advice was needed, requiring insight and wisdom."

Belshazzar asked Daniel, as he stood before him, "They say you advised my father the king.
My wise men have tried to read the inscription, but they can not tell me what it means."

The king said, "I have sought soothsayers, and sent for the wise men to come.
They can not tell me what this writing is, or give me the

interpretation thereof."

"A gold chain I will put around your neck. I will dress you in purple linen.
I will give you great authority Daniel, even to third highest in the kingdom."

Daniel answered, "You may keep your gifts, however, I will read this writing to the King.
The inscription and its interpretation, I will tell you what it means."

"The holy vessels from the temple of God, crafted in silver and gold,
You brought them to worship your foreign gods, made from bronze, wood, iron and stone."

"The golden goblets held in the treasury, Nebuchadnezzar took from Jerusalem.
You defied God so your nobles and wives might drink their wine from them!"

"This is the message that was written:
Mene, Mene, Tekel, and Parsin
This is what these words mean:"

"Mene means numbered—God has numbered the days of your reign and has brought it to an end.
Tekel means weighed—you have been weighed on the balances and have not measured up.
Parsin means divided—your kingdom is divided, given to the Medes and Persians."

A gold chain was put around Daniels neck. The King dressed him in purple and linen.
Gave him the position of authority, even to third highest in the kingdom.

That night Belshazzar was killed and this Babylonian king's reign was through.
Darius the Mede took the kingdom for Persia at age of sixty-two.

DANIEL IN THE LIONS' DEN

DANIEL IN THE LIONS' DEN

King Darius appointed officials and put them in charge over the land.
Three more were set above all these, the greatest, Daniel, was his friend.

These men were appointed so the King could rest. They put his mind at ease,
So he could tend to more important matters such as writing kingly decrees.

King Darius had confidence in Daniel, his spirit a trusted friend.
He set Daniel over the entire kingdom with no one higher than him.

These officials were jealous of Daniel, his position given by the king.
They tried to make trouble for Daniel, tried to find him in some corrupt thing.

Daniel was trustworthy and faithful, no corruption could be found.
"None of us will increase in rank as long as this man is around."

The men said we cannot find any fault, in Daniel there appears no fraud,
Unless we can find another way in regard to Daniel's religion or his God.

These officers created a plan, so they all came in together,
To consult with the King exclaiming praise, "May Darius our king live forever!"

"A law need be written that requires your signet ring.
For thirty days no one can pray, except pray you, oh King."

"Your majesty write the decree, to all your provinces we will send.
If anyone dare be found guilty, he will be thrown in the lion's den."

Darius replied, "In respect to Mede and Persia, I think this law is fine."
Daniel went inside his house when he learned this decree was signed.

Daniel's upper room had windows that faced Jerusalem as he prayed.
Daniel did as he always had. He prayed to God three times a day.

They burst in and found Daniel seeking help, praying to his God.
They arrested Daniel and went to the King and asked him about this law.

"Didn't you just sign a law forbidding prayer to anyone but you?"
Darius replied, "The decree stands, yes what you say is true."

"Daniel, this exile from Judah, pays no attention your

majesty.

He is still praying three times a day, ignoring your law's decree."

When the King heard this report he was extremely sad and dismayed.

He did everything he could until sunset, to try to save Daniel that day.

The men came in together and said this law cannot be changed.

After all, this was the plan. They had it prearranged.

So the king gave the order to get Daniel, and by law cast him in.

"May the God you serve continually, Daniel, save you from the lions' den."

A stone was rolled over the top, set in place and it was sealed.

Now no one could rescue Daniel, to make sure that he was killed.

The King was sad and would not eat. No sleep was found in this night.

The King rushed to the lions' den as the sun rose, with first sign of light.

"Daniel, servant of the living God all night long I have prayed.

Please tell me you are still alive, you from the lions God has saved."

After being thrown into the lion's den, King Darius prayed to God for Daniel's safety. God protected Daniel by sending an angel to watch over him.

Daniel then answered, "I'm here oh King. My God sent an angel to shut their jaws.
I am safe because I'm innocent. I have done nothing wrong."

The King ordered Daniel lifted out, not a wound or a scratch could be found.
Darius wrote to the nations in every language, "May you prosper and with peace abound."

"Men are to tremble before Daniel's God, who performed signs and wonders across this land.
He is the living God. He is all powerful, able to save Daniel from the lions' den."

BOOK OF JONAH

BOOK OF JONAH

⚜

God spoke to Jonah, told him, "Get up and arise.
Go to the great city Nineveh, there you shall prophesy."

"Cry out against it Jonah, for their wickedness is great."
Jonah got up, ran the other direction, trying to get away!

He went to the port of Joppa, bought a ticket and paid the
fare.
The ship was headed to Tarshish. He would escape God by
fleeing there.

The LORD caused a powerful storm, to hurl upon the sea.
It threatened to break the ship apart, as the wind blew
violently.

The sailors all prayed to their gods, afraid, fearing for their
lives.
Together they worked to lighten the load, throwing cargo
over the side.

Jonah fast asleep in the hold, the captain found him that way.
He shouted at Jonah, "How can you sleep? You had better get
up and pray!"

"Maybe your God will pay attention. If you pray, he might
just save our lives.
Let us cast lots, to find him responsible, for this storm's
sudden uprise."

The lots were cast and fell on Jonah, he told them he was on the run.
"Who are you? What is your line of work? What country are you from?"

Jonah answered, "I am Hebrew, my God is the God of heaven. He made the sea and land."
The sailors were terrified when they heard this, powerfully delivered into his hand.

They asked, "Why are you running away?" and then, "Why did you do it?
What shall we do now, to stop this storm? Why are you putting us through this?"

Jonah said, "It's all my fault. It's just as terrible as it could be. In order to make the storm be calm, you must throw me into the sea."

The sailors rowed even harder, trying to get the ship to land.
They rowed but couldn't make it, the storm was just too strong for them.

To Jonah's God, "O LORD, they prayed, don't let us die for his sin.
Do not put innocent blood on us, for we are going to throw him in."

They picked up Jonah together, and threw him into the sea.
As soon as Jonah hit the water the storm stopped immediately.

When the sailors saw the power of Jonah's God, they vowed

and sacrificed.
The LORD made a great fish swallow Jonah, him inside three days and three nights.

Inside the fish, Jonah prayed to God, asked to be saved and see land.
Then the LORD gave orders to the fish, to retch up Jonah on dry sand.

God spoke to Jonah, told him, "Get up and arise!
Go to the great city Nineveh. There you shall prophesy.

"Cry out against it Jonah, for their wickedness is great."
Jonah got up and praised the LORD, this time Jonah obeyed!

Jonah said, "I will do whatever you tell me to do."
The city of Nineveh was very large, it took three days to walk through.

Jonah prophesied out loud in the city, "Soon you will all be overthrown."
Believing Jonah they all repented, from the least to the king on the throne.

The King believed what Jonah told him, put on sackcloth, took off his royal robes.
Then he sent a decree into the city, every noble in the land to be told.

"Nobody is allowed to eat or drink. When they are hungry, tell them to pray.
They must repent, end their violence, and turn from their wicked ways."

After being swallowed by a whale, Jonah prayed to God to be
saved. God ordered the whale to spit Jonah up on dry sand.
He then commanded Jonah to go to Nineveh and prophesy.

God saw that they were sorry, so he waited, and held back the devastation he declared.
All that was coming against them, they repented and were spared!

Jonah got very angry, to him this just seemed wrong.
This change of plans upset him greatly, it was only going to prolong.

"That's why I ran to Tarshish, I knew you would do this.
So full of mercy and compassion, why did you put me through this?"

Jonah said, "If what I predicted will not happen, LORD, I'd rather be dead than alive."
The LORD said, "Do you have good reason to be angry, if I let these people survive?"

Jonah went out of the city, climbed onto a cliff facing east.
There he made himself a shelter. It was nice in the shade at least.

God arranged for a leafy plant, Jonah was thankful and pleased.
The plant grew over Jonah's head, so his discomfort eased.

Scorching east wind, the sun beat down, when dawn came the next day.
Then God sent a worm to eat the plant. It died and withered away.

God asked Jonah, "Do you have good cause to be angry about the plant?"
He said, "Yes even unto death, under the circumstance."

"You feel sorry about the plant, though you did nothing to put it there.
Nineveh has 120,000 living souls Jonah, should I just not care?"

God provided Jonah with a leafy plant to ease his discomfort.

THE BIRTH OF JESUS

THE BIRTH OF JESUS

This is the story of how our Savior came down here to
Earth.
Jesus the son of Mary crowned Messiah at his birth.

God sent the angel Gabriel to the city of Galilee.
To the virgin Mary, told her she was favored mightily.

"Do not be afraid Mary. God's favor you have won.
You will become pregnant and you will bear a son."

Mary asked, "How can this be, as I have not known any
man?"
"Only believe that this is possible, for God has a great plan."

"The power of the most high God will overshadow and shine
through.
This holy Child of God, in purity will come through you."

"The Son of the most high God, will grow to be a great Man.
The throne of his ancestor David, and his kingdom, will never
end."

Mary said, "I am the Lord's servant. Let all you say happen to
me."
Mary was promised to Joseph, and then he had a dream:

The angel said, "Do not be afraid Joseph, to take Mary as
your wife.

The angel Gabriel appears before the virgin Mary informing
her that she will be become pregnant and will have a son.

For what is conceived in her womb has from the Holy Spirit
been given life."

Fulfilling Isaiah's prophecy: "Behold a virgin giving birth to
a son."
The Christ, he is the Messiah, the one prophesied to come.

Now in those days Caesar Augustus sent forth a decree:
The entire Roman world must be accounted for individually.

Everyone required to register—each to their own land.
Joseph went from Nazareth in Galilee to Judea in Bethlehem.

Joseph had to travel, he from the house of David's line.
Together with Mary, pregnant and very close to the time.

In Bethlehem her labor began. The baby was going to come.
She had to try to find a safe place to give birth to her son.

The town of Bethlehem was full. They had no rooms left for a
stranger.
Jesus was born, wrapped in swaddling cloth, and Mary laid
him in a manger.

Nearby the local shepherds were watching their flocks at
night.
An angel appeared before them shone with a glorious
bright light.

"Do not be afraid for I am bringing you great news full of
joy!
In the town of David born tonight you will find a baby boy."

"He is the awaited Messiah. He is the anointed LORD.
Unto you this night a Savior in Bethlehem has been born."

Suddenly a great company of angels appeared, praising God
singing blessed.
"Glory to God in the highest heaven, peace on whom His
favor rests."

Then the angels left, went back to heaven. The shepherd's
said to one another,
"Let's go quickly to Bethlehem to find this child and his
mother."

They went and found the child, hearts rejoicing full of hope
and cheer.
They told Mary and Joseph what the angels said when they
did appear!

Mary's heart was full, as she pondered and treasured up all of
these things.
This baby boy she held in her arms—Almighty God, "The
King of Kings."

THE STORY OF LAZARUS

THE STORY OF LAZARUS

Mary and Martha were sisters. They lived in Bethany. They sent a message to Jesus pleading, "LORD come quickly!"

This Mary anointed Jesus with perfume costly and rare.
She dried and wiped off Jesus' feet using her own hair.

Martha and Mary's brother Lazarus had become very sick.
They sent a word by messenger telling Jesus to "Come quick,

"To care for our brother Lazarus, the one whom you love.
Oh please Rabbi to us now hurry and come!"

Jesus said, "Lazarus' sickness will not be his end."
He loved them dearly in his heart. They were Jesus' closest friends.

Even after hearing the news, two more days he stayed.
He said to his disciples, "Time to go, we must go back to Judea."

The disciples cried, "They tried to stone you, you cannot go back again!"
Jesus said, "Lazarus is sleeping and we must go and wake up our friend.

"There are 12 hours in a day. The righteous can walk in the light.
But all the wicked who walk in darkness will stumble in the

night."

They did not know it was to honor God, and promote his Son in glory.
They thought it was a natural sleep the way Jesus told the story.

Jesus said, "Lazarus is dead, for your sake I was not there to receive.
God will further show you His glory and it will help you to believe."

Thomas the twin said to the disciples, "Let us too go there and die."
Lazarus had been 4 days in the tomb, dead when Jesus arrived.

Bethany was near Jerusalem only about two miles away.
A good number of Jews came out to comfort Mary and Martha that day.

Martha learned Jesus was coming. She ran and Mary stayed behind.
Martha said, "If you had only been here, my brother wouldn't have died."

"Even now, what you ask from God, he will give to you,"
Jesus said. "Your brother will rise again, do you believe this is true?"

Martha said, "I know in the resurrection he will rise again that day.
All that believe and trust in you will never really pass away."

Jesus said, "I AM the resurrection. I AM the truth and the life. Whoever believes and trusts in me will truly never die."

He asked Martha, "Do you believe this?" She said, "LORD I have always believed.
I will continue to have this faith. It is you in whom I cleave."

"You are the beloved Son of God, into this world you have come.
You are the Christ, the Messiah. You are the Anointed One."

Martha left and went to Mary said, "The Rabbi has asked you come."
And when Mary heard this she sprang up quickly. To Jesus she would run.

Jesus had not yet come into the village. So Martha brought her to his place.
The Jews in the house with Mary, saw her leave with great haste.

They followed after her, supposing she had gone to the tomb, to pour out her heart and grieve there.
Mary came and dropped at Jesus feet crying, "My LORD if you had only been here."

Jesus saw Mary was weeping, and the Jews that were with her were crying.
They said, "He who opened a blind man's eyes, but couldn't keep His friend from dying."

Jesus asked, "Where have you laid him?" They said, "LORD come and see."
He was deeply moved in his spirit. He sighed and cried with grief.

Jesus wept. As he approached the tomb he said, "Roll the stone away!"
Martha said, "The smell will be bad. LORD he's been in there dead for four days."

"For the promise of God the Father, The Glory of God you will see."
Jesus said, "Did I not promise you he would rise again, if you only would believe?"

So together they rolled away the stone, Jesus lifted his eyes and prayed,
"Father God I know you hear me, on account of the people this day,"

"For them to know you did send me, and in their hearts hold no more doubt."
He shouted with a loud voice and said, "LAZARUS come forth and come out!!!"

The Jews who had come there with Mary, upon seeing what Jesus had done,
Believed and received him with all of their hearts. Their faith had greatly been won.

Then out came Lazarus walking. The man who four days had been dead!
Tearing off the burial cloth still bound and wrapped up on his

head!

The Jews who had buried Lazarus knew he was dead and was gone.
In shock they ran to the Pharisees and told them what Jesus had done.

After moving away the tombstone, Jesus commanded
"Lazarus come forth and come out!" Lazarus came walking
out to Jesus and the crowd after being dead for four days.

MARY HEART MARTHA WORLD

A MARY HEART IN A MARTHA WORLD

Jesus and his disciples were coming to town.
Everywhere they went a crowd gathered around.

Martha was frantic, her Lord was so near.
Mary yelled he's coming, he's coming, the Lord's almost here !

Her house must look perfect, her food I delight.
There was so much to do, she wanted it right.

She wished she could be out with them having fun.
When Jesus arrived, still so much to be done.

Where is Mary, where is she ? there's work to complete.
Mary was sitting down at the Lord's feet.

Martha thought it was not fair,
Her sister Mary should do her share.

My Lord came Martha to Jesus and said,
There is still much to be done before we will be fed.

Make her get up and do her share.
I'm doing all the work you don't think that's fair ?

Mary was getting spiritually fed,
Martha chose to serve instead.

What we think is right is often not,
We must consider the time that we've got.

The harvest is full, the field is ripe
We must work by day while we still have the light.

Drink the water he gives and never again thirst ?
I think what he's saying, is we must put him first.

He didn't say Martha was doing wrong,
He only said Mary was where she belonged.

He said see to my sheep, See to it they are fed.
That one of the last things that the Lord ever said ….

Jesus visits with Mary and Martha. During His visit, Martha spends time preparing the house and keeping busy, while Mary spends time with Jesus.

PETER IN CHAINS

PETER IN CHAINS

Now Herod persecuted the church of God. He had James
put to death with a sword.
Violently seized all who belonged to the church, all the
disciples who called Jesus LORD.

When Herod saw that this pleased the Jews, he arrested Peter
as well.
They caught Peter and threw him in prison, and assigned four
guards to his cell.

Peter was chained between two soldiers, night before Herod
brought his case.
While Peter was held the church fervently prayed, "God, keep
Peter safe."

Behold, an angel of the LORD appeared suddenly. A light
shone in the cell.
"Get up quickly!" An angel struck Peter's side, and off of his
hands the chains fell.

The angel said to him, "Put on your sandals, wrap your coat
around, follow me."
He went out, followed, though he didn't know if this was real.
Or was he having a dream?

They passed the first guard, then second guard, and came to
the big iron gate.
Suddenly, click! the gate opened itself. Immediately the angel
went away.

An angel of the LORD appears to Peter while he is in
prison. The angel strikes Peter to wake him and the chains
fell off of Peter's hands. Miraculously, they leave the
prison without waking any guards.

When Peter came to himself, he said, "I know for sure, that the LORD has sent this forth.
The LORD sent his angel to rescue me! It was an angel who opened those doors!"

"From the hand of Herod, this angel saved me. I'm free, my hands are unbound!"
When he realized this, went to the house of Mary, where all the church gathered around.

Peter knocked at the door. A servant girl came—she did not open, made him wait.
She ran quickly and announced to all inside, "It is Peter standing at the gate."

They said to her, "You are out of your mind!" She kept insisting that she was sure.
Peter continued knocking. They thought it his angel, and then they opened the door.

With his hand he motioned to quiet them down. He told how the angel lead his escape.
Peter told them, "Report these things to my brothers and sisters," then he left for another place.

The next morning there was no small disturbance. The soldiers asked what happened, and why?
Herod searched for Peter. When he could not be found, ordered the guards sent to die.

THE ROAD TO DAMASCUS

THE ROAD TO DAMASCUS

Saul was still raging with threats of murder, against the people of The Way.
Went to the high priest, seeking authority, for a letter that would convey

Authorization to bring back to the city any Christ followers found—
Man or woman, the permission to bring these prisoners back tied and bound.

As he traveled approaching Damascus, a light from heaven came suddenly.
Flashing as it encircled him, "Saul, Saul why are you persecuting me?"

Saul fell to the ground saying, "Who are you, LORD? Only tell me please!"
He said, "I AM Jesus. The one that you are persecuting is me."

"Now get up. Enter the city. You will be told what you must do."
The men that were with him saw nothing, but did hear the voice speaking too.

Saul got up from the ground. His eyes were open, but he could not see.
His men had to lead him into Damascus by the hand. The days that passed numbered three.

As Saul heads to Damascus to bring back and execute Christians, a light from heaven shines around him and he falls to the ground. The LORD speaks to him and asks him why he is persecuting Him?

In Damascus the LORD spoke to Ananias, told him in a
vision of the befall.
"Go to the house of Judas. Find a man there from Tarsus
called Saul."

"In a vision I have shown him Ananias, that you would come,
lay hands on him.
He is praying for me to help him, that he might recover his
sight again."

But Ananias answered, "LORD, I have heard much about this
man,
How much harm he did to your saints, down in Jerusalem."

"Here he has authority from the high priests to bind all who
call on your name."
The LORD said, "Go. He is my chosen instrument, appointed
to proclaim."

"I've selected him to bear my name, to Israel, gentiles and
kings.
For my name's sake Ananias, he will endure much suffering."

Ananias obeyed and entered the house, laid his hands upon
Saul's head.
"Brother Saul, the LORD Jesus appeared to you, on the road
which you were led."

"He has sent me that you may be filled with the Spirit, and
again regain your sight."
Immediately scales fell from Saul's eyes and he was able
again to see light.

He took food and was strengthened, then got up and was baptized.

All these things he never knew, he finally realized.

www.ingramcontent.com/pod-product-compliance
Lightning Source LLC
Chambersburg PA
CBHW020512030426
42337CB00011B/346